1,000,000 Books

are available to read at

Forgotten Books

www.ForgottenBooks.com

Read online
Download PDF
Purchase in print

ISBN 978-1-333-03339-2
PIBN 10456074

This book is a reproduction of an important historical work. Forgotten Books uses state-of-the-art technology to digitally reconstruct the work, preserving the original format whilst repairing imperfections present in the aged copy. In rare cases, an imperfection in the original, such as a blemish or missing page, may be replicated in our edition. We do, however, repair the vast majority of imperfections successfully; any imperfections that remain are intentionally left to preserve the state of such historical works.

Forgotten Books is a registered trademark of FB &c Ltd.
Copyright © 2018 FB &c Ltd.
FB &c Ltd, Dalton House, 60 Windsor Avenue, London, SW19 2RR.
Company number 08720141. Registered in England and Wales.

For support please visit www.forgottenbooks.com

1 MONTH OF FREE READING

at

www.ForgottenBooks.com

By purchasing this book you are eligible for one month membership to ForgottenBooks.com, giving you unlimited access to our entire collection of over 1,000,000 titles via our web site and mobile apps.

To claim your free month visit:

www.forgottenbooks.com/free456074

* Offer is valid for 45 days from date of purchase. Terms and conditions apply.

English
Français
Deutsche
Italiano
Español
Português

www.forgottenbooks.com

Mythology Photography **Fiction**
Fishing Christianity **Art** Cooking
Essays Buddhism Freemasonry
Medicine **Biology** Music **Ancient Egypt** Evolution Carpentry Physics
Dance Geology **Mathematics** Fitness
Shakespeare **Folklore** Yoga Marketing
Confidence Immortality Biographies
Poetry **Psychology** Witchcraft
Electronics Chemistry History **Law**
Accounting **Philosophy** Anthropology
Alchemy Drama Quantum Mechanics
Atheism Sexual Health **Ancient History**
Entrepreneurship Languages Sport
Paleontology Needlework Islam
Metaphysics Investment Archaeology
Parenting Statistics Criminology
Motivational

CONSTITUTION

AND

BY-LAWS

OF THE

NEW JERSEY HISTORICAL SOCIETY.

REVISED MAY 20, 1897.

NEWARK, N. J.:
PRINTED BY WARD & TICHENOR, 832 & 834 BROAD STREET.
1897.

AN ACT TO INCORPORATE THE NEW JERSEY HISTORICAL SOCIETY.

WHEREAS the persons herein after named, and others, have formed themselves into an association, under the name and title of "the New Jersey Historical Society," the object of which society is "to discover, procure and preserve whatever relates to any department of the history of New Jersey, natural, civil, literary, or ecclesiastical. and generally of other portions of the United States;" and whereas the said society has, by its executive committee, presented a memorial to the legislature, praying for an act of incorporation, that the purposes of said society may be the more effectually subserved— therefore,

1. Be it enacted by the Senate and General Assembly of the State of New Jersey, That Daniel V. McLean, Peter D Vroom, Eli F. Cooley, Amzi C. McLean, Richard S. Field, Stacy G. Potts, Henry W. Green, Aaron A. Marcelus, Nicholas Murray, William P. Robeson, William B. Kinney, Thomas Gordon, James T. Sherman, William A. Whitehead, George W. Doane, and their associates, who now are, and such other persons as shall hereafter become members of the said society, shall be, and are hereby ordained, constituted, and declared a body corporate and politic, by the name of "the New Jersey Historical Society"; and that, by that name, they and their successors for ever hereafter shall and may have succession, and, by the same name, be capable in law to sue and be sued, plead and be impleaded. answer and be answered unto, defend and be defended, in all courts of law and equity, in all manner of actions, suits,

complaints, and matters whatsoever; and that they and their successors may have a common seal, and the same break, alter, change and renew at their pleasure; and, by the same, shall be for ever hereafter capable in law to purchase, take, hold, receive, and enjoy, to them and their successors, any lands, tenements, hereditaments, goods, chattels, or estate, real or personal, of whatever nature or quality, in fee simple, for life or lives, or for years, or in any other manner whatsoever; provided always, that the yearly income or value of the said real or personal estate, or both, do not at any time exceed the sum of two thousand dollars.

2. And be it enacted, That they and their successors shall, by the same name, have power and authority to give, grant, bargain, sell. demise, release, and convey to others the whole or any part of such real or personal estate, on such terms and in such manner and form as the said society may deem eligible to subserve and promote the purposes and design of said society; and that they and their successors shall have power, from time to time, to abolish any of the offices or appointments herein after mentioned, and create others in their room, with such powers and duties as they may think fit to confer and prescribe, and shall have power, from time to time, to make, constitute, and ordain such constitution, by-laws, ordinances, and regulations as they shall judge proper for the election of officers, the election and admission of new members, for the government and regulation of the officers and members, for fixing the times and places of the meetings of the said corporation, and the same, from time to time, to alter, change, repeal, revoke, and annul, at their pleasure; and that the constitution and by-laws, rules and regulations, of the society heretofore made and adopted, and now existing, shall and may remain in

force until altered or repealed by the said corporation; provided, that such by-laws and constitution, made, or to be made, by the said corporation, shall not be repugnant to the constitution and laws of the United States or of this State.

3. And be it enacted, That this act shall be, and is hereby declared to be a public act, and shall be construed most favorably to promote the purposes and designs of the said society; and that no misnomer of the said corporation, in any deed, will, testament, gift, grant, demise or other instrument of contract or conveyance, shall vitiate or defeat the same; provided the said corporation shall be sufficiently described to show the intention of the parties.

4. And be it enacted, That this act shall be and remain in full force until the year of our Lord one thousand nine hundred; provided nevertheless, that in case the aforesaid society shall at any time appropriate their, or any part of their funds to any purpose or purposes other than those contemplated by this act, and shall be thereof convicted by due course of law, that thenceforth the said corporation shall cease and determine, and the estate, real and personal, whereof it may be seized and possessed shall vest in the people of this State.

Approved, February 6, 1846.

A SUPPLEMENT TO THE ACT ENTITLED "AN ACT TO INCORPORATE THE NEW JERSEY HISTORICAL SOCIETY."

1. BE IT ENACTED by the Senate and General Assembly of the State of New Jersey, That no state, county, city, ward, township or other public assessments, taxes or charges whatsoever, shall at any time be levied or imposed upon the said society, or upon the stocks,

estates, lands or tenements which have become or may become vested in them by virtue of the act by which they were incorporated, so long as said society shall appropriate and use the whole of their income to promote the objects set forth in the said act of incorporation; provided always, that the yearly income of the said real or personal estate, or both, do not at any one time exceed the sum of five thousand dollars.

Approved, March 6, 1856.

AN ACT AUTHORIZING THE EXTENSION OF THE CHARTERS OF LITERARY, HISTORICAL, GENEALOGICAL, LIBRARY OR SCIENTIFIC SOCIETIES, INCORPORATED BY OR UNDER ANY LAW OF THIS STATE.

1. BE IT ENACTED by the Senate and General Assembly of the State of New Jersey, That it shall be lawful for any literary, historical, genealogical, library or scientific society heretofore or hereafter created under or by virtue of any law of this state, to adopt a resolution at the regular annual meeting of such society, declaring that it is the desire and purpose of such society to extend its charter beyond the time limited in the act or certificate of incorporation of such society, which resolution shall also specify the term for which such society desires and proposes that its charter shall be extended, not exceeding fifty years from and beyond the time limited as aforesaid; and whenever a copy of such resolution, certified under the hand of its president, and under its common seal, attested by its recording secretary, shall be filed in the office of the secretary of state of this state, the charter of such society shall thereupon and thereby be extended for and during the term specified in such resolution.

Approved March 10, 1893.

WHEREAS, The New Jersey Historical Society was incorporated by act of the Legislature, approved February 6, 1846, and in and by such act of incorporation it was provided that said act should be and remain in force until the year of our Lord one thousand nine hundred;

AND WHEREAS, by an act entitled "An Act authorizing the extension of the charters of literary, historical, genealogical, library and scientific societies, incorporated by or under the laws of this State," approved March 10, 1893, it is provided: "That it shall be lawful for any literary, historical, genealogical, library or scientific society heretofore or hereafter created under or by virtue of any law of this state, to adopt a resolution at the regular annual meeting of such society, declaring that it is the desire and purpose of such society to extend its charter beyond the time limited in the act or certificate of incorporation of such society, which resolution shall also specify the term for which such society desires and proposes that its charter shall be extended, not exceeding fifty years from and beyond the time limited as aforesaid,"

RESOLVED, That The New Jersey Historical Society, incorporated by act of the Legislature of this State, approved February sixth, one thousand eight hundred and forty-six, hereby declares that it is the desire and purpose of such Society to extend its charter for the term of fifty years from and beyond the time limited in the act of incorporation of such Society.

RESOLVED, That a copy of the foregoing resolution certified under the hand of the President; and under the common seal of the Society, attested by the Recording Secretary, shall be filed in the office of the Secretary of State of this State, to the end that the charter of this Society shall be extended for the term of fifty years from and beyond the time limited in its charter as aforesaid. Attested:

ERNEST E. COE,   S. H PENNINGTON,
Recording Secretary.   *President*, [L. S.]

Endorsed, " Filed June 5, 1894,
    HENRY C KELSEY,
        Secretary of State."

STATE OF NEW JERSEY,

DEPARTMENT OF STATE.

I, ALEXANDER H. RICKEY, Assistant Secretary of State of the State of New Jersey, do hereby Certify, that the foregoing is a true copy of Certificate of Extension of Charter of The New Jersey Historical Society, and the endorsement thereon as the same is taken from and compared with the original filed in the office of the Secretary of State on the 5th day of June, A.D., 1894, and now remaining on file therein.

In Testimony Whereof, I have hereunto set my hand and affixed my Official Seal, at Trenton, this fourth day of February, A.D., 1897.

        A. H. RICKEY,
[Seal.]   *Assistant Secretary of State.*

The Committee appointed at the meeting of the New Jersey Historical Society, held at Trenton on Tuesday, January 26, 1897, to revise the Constitution and By-Laws of the Society, report and recommend the following:

CONSTITUTION.

ARTICLE I.

This Society shall be called the New Jersey Historical Society, and shall be located in the city of Newark. Its object shall be to discover, procure, and preserve whatever relates to any department of the history of New Jersey, natural, civil, literary or ecclesiastical, and generally of other portions of the United States.

ARTICLE II.

This Society shall consist of Life, Contributing, Corresponding and Honorary Members and Patrons. Life and Contributing Members and Patrons only shall be entitled to vote and hold office. Residents of New Jersey shall not be elected Corresponding Members. Not more than five Honorary Members shall be elected in any one year.

ARTICLE III.

The Officers of this Society shall be a President, First, Second and Third Vice-Presidents, a Corresponding Secretary, Recording Secretary, and Treasurer, who shall be, *ex officio*, Members of the Board of Trustees. The Officers shall be elected by the Board of Trustees, within thirty days after each Annual Meeting, and shall hold office until their successors are elected. The Board of Trustees shall fill vacancies.

Article IV.

At the next Annual Meeting there shall be elected fifteen Trustees, five to serve one year, five to serve two years and five to serve three years, or until their successors are elected, and thereafter, at each Annual Meeting, five Trustees shall be elected, to serve for three years, or until their successors are elected. Upon the death, resignation, refusal to act, or cessation of membership in the Society, of any Trustee, or the election of a Trustee to any other Office in the Society, or the unexcused failure, of any Trustee, to attend four successive regular Meetings of the Board, his office shall be deemed vacant, and the Board may appoint a Member to fill the vacancy until the next Annual Meeting, when a Trustee shall be elected for the unexpired term. The Board of Trustees shall report to the Society at each Annual Meeting.

Article V.

There shall be a Committee on Genealogy and Statistics, to consist of one Member from each County of the State, of whom five shall constitute a quorum; also a Committee on Colonial Documents, to consist of five Members; which Committees, with such other Committees as may be required, shall be appointed annually by the President, who may fill vacancies at any time. All Committees shall report to the Society at each Annual Meeting.

Article VI.

Contributing Members shall pay Five Dollars annually, or, upon the payment of Fifty Dollars at any one time, any person, approved by the Board of Trustees, may on request become a Life Member, and shall be exempt from annual dues; and every Member, who shall have paid the annual dues for twenty years successively, shall thereafter on request be a Life Member Failure by any Contributing Member to pay his annual dues for three years, or refusal on notice to pay the same, shall involve forfeiture of all the privileges of membership, and the name of such Member may be erased from the List of Members by vote of the Board of Trustees. This article shall not apply to or affect any person now a Life Member of the Society. Any person may become a Patron of the Society by contributing One Thousand Dollars to its treasury at any one time, and his certificate as such Patron shall be transferable, but every such transfer must be approved by the Board of Trustees. Patrons shall be entitled to a copy of all publications of the Society.

Article VII.

The Board of Trustees shall have the full and exclusive control of all the trust funds derived from donations, bequests, and life memberships, and of all other property, real and personal, belonging to the Society, and shall have the management of all the financial affairs of the Society. All donations and bequests of money made to this Society shall be held in trust for the uses and purposes designated by the donors, and no part of the principal sum of any trust fund, or any moneys received from Life Memberships, shall ever be used in payment of the current annual expenditures of the Society. All moneys appropriated by any public body or society, or by any person, and intrusted to this Society, or to any of its Officers or Committees, shall forthwith be turned over to the Treasurer.

ARTICLE VIII.

The location of the Library and Cabinet of the Society shall not at any time be changed, from one municipality to another, except by an affirmative vote of two-thirds of the Members present at any Meeting of the Society; notice of which proposed change must be given in writing to the Board of Trustees or to the Society at least two months before action thereon; and such change shall not take effect, unless approved in writing by two thirds of the Board of Trustees.

ARTICLE IX.

This Constitution may be altered or amended by an affirmative vote of two-thirds of the Members present at any Meeting of the Society, provided the same shall have been proposed in writing to the Board of Trustees or to the Society at least two months previous to such Meeting; and such alteration or amendment shall not take effect, unless approved in writing by two-thirds of the Board of Trustees.

BY=LAWS.

I. The Election of Members shall be by vote of the Board of Trustees, to whom all applications and nominations for membership and all resignations of membership shall be referred with power.

II. The Annual Meeting of the Society shall be held on the last Wednesday in October, at such place and hour as the Society, or, on its failure to act, as its Board of Trustees may from time to time appoint. Such other Meetings may be held as the Board of Trustees may appoint, at such times and places as they may designate; at which Meetings, besides the regular business, or social exercises, addresses may be delivered and historical papers read, before the Society, by persons selected by the Board of Trustees.

III. Fifteen Members of the Society shall constitute a quorum, for the transaction of business; excepting when charges against a Trustee or Officer are to be disposed of, or an amendment to the Constitution or By-Laws, or a change of location of the Library or Cabinet is to be acted on, when fifty must be present.

IV. At Meetings of the Society, the following shall be the Order of Business:
1. Reading Minutes of last Meeting.
2. Report of Corresponding Secretary.
3. Report of Treasurer.
4. Report of Board of Trustees.
5. Reports of Committees.
6 Report of Librarian.
7. Communications from other Societies.
8. Miscellaneous Business.
9. Papers and Addresses.

This Order of Business may at any time be dispensed with or altered by a majority of the Members present and voting.

V. The President, one of the Vice-Presidents, ,or a Chairman, *pro tem.*, shall preside at all Meetings of the Society, and shall have a casting vote. The President shall appoint all Committees not otherwise provided for; and shall exercise and maintain a general supervision over the affairs of the Society, see that its object, as prescribed by the Constitution, is duly carried out, and take an active interest in all that pertains to the welfare of the Society. The Vice-Presidents, in their order, shall, in the absence or disability of the President, perform the duties of that Officer.

VI. The Corresponding Secretary shall have the temporary custody of all letters and communications to the Society. He may, at the Meetings, read such letters and communications as he may have received, and shall prepare all letters connected with the business or object of the Society, excepting such as may be referred to, or may relate to the duties of any Committee. All original letters, communications and manuscripts, in possession of the Board of Trustees or of any Committee, shall be delivered to the Corresponding Secretary, and shall be by him forthwith deposited in the Library, copies only being retained if necessary. He shall notify all Members of their election, and of such other matters as he may deem necessary, or be directed to communicate ; and shall keep, in suitable books to be provided for the purpose, copies of all important letters written on behalf of the Society. He shall carefully preserve the originals of all letters and other communications he may receive, and shall forthwith deposit the same in the Library, retaining copies if necessary. He shall also be the Corresponding Secretary of the Board of Trustees.

VII. The Recording Secretary shall have charge of the Constitution, By-Laws and Records of the Society. He shall keep a fair and accurate Record of the Proceedings of the Society, in a book provided for the purpose, the same to be kept in an appointed place in the Library, convenient of access by the Board of Trustees or any Committee. He shall give notice to the several Officers, Board of Trustees, or Committees, of all votes, orders, resolves and proceedings of the Society, affecting them, or appertaining to their respective duties. He shall also send, by mail, a notice of the time and place of each Meeting of the Society, two weeks previously, to each Life and Contributing Member and Patron. If two months' notice has been given of any proposed alteration or amendment of the Constitution or By-Laws, or of any change of location of the Library or Cabinet of the Society, the fact shall be stated in the notice of the Meeting following the expiration of said two months. He shall, after each Meeting of the Society or Board of Trustees, forthwith deposit in the Library all papers read and copies of addresses delivered before the Society, together with the originals of all notices, propositions and resolutions, retaining copies if necessary. He shall also be the Recording Secretary of the Board of Trustees

VIII. The Treasurer shall collect and keep the funds and securities of the Society; and, as often as these funds shall amount to Twenty Dollars, they shall be deposited in some bank (approved by the Trustees) to the credit of the New Jersey Historical Society, and shall be drawn thence on the check of the Treasurer, for the purposes following only. Out of these funds he shall pay such sums as may be ordered by the Board of Trustees, or by any Committee, from the funds in their care, respectively He shall keep a true account of the receipts and payments, and shall render a monthly statement of the same to the Board of Trustees, and an annual statement to the Society. In case of temporary disability of the Treasurer, the Board of Trustees may appoint a Treasurer, *pro tem*.

IX. It shall be the duty of the Board of Trustees to recommend plans for promoting its object; to digest and prepare business; to authorize the disbursement and expenditure of the annual income and other moneys of the Society, or so much thereof as shall be needed for the payment of salaries, current expenses, fitting up the Library, the ordinary purchase of books, binding, printing, and other necessary outlays; but in no case to exceed the funds in hand, or to anticipate the income of any one year. They shall have power to employ a Librarian and such other persons as may be necessary for the proper administration of the affairs of the Society, and to prescribe their duties and fix their salaries. They shall have charge of the arrangement and regulation of the Library and Cabinet; and shall, from time to time, examine into the condition of the same, and into the state of the finances; and shall generally superintend the interests of the Society, and execute all such duties as may from time to time be committed to them. They shall keep a record of all their proceedings, and make a report at each Annual Meeting of the Society. They shall meet statedly for the transaction of business, once at least in each month. From their number the President shall appoint Committees, annually, of three Members each, on Finance, on Library, on Printing, on Membership, and on Building; which Committees shall attend to the duties delegated to them, and report monthly to the Board. At all Meetings of the Board of Trustees, five Members shall constitute a quorum for the transaction of business. The President of the Society shall be President of the Board of Trustees, and the Corresponding and Recording Secretaries of the Society shall be respectively he Corresponding and Recording Secretaries of the Board of Trustees. The Recording Secretary shall be *ex officio* a member of the Committee on Printing.

X. It shall be the duty of the Committee on Genealogy and Statistics to arrange all genealogical and statistical data in the possession of the Society, and furnish information, as far as possible, to all inquirers on such subjects. The originals of all letters asking, and copies of all letters giving such information, shall be delivered to the Corresponding Secretary, and shall be by him forthwith deposited in the Library.

XI. The following shall be the regulations for the use of the Library:

1. No book or manuscript shall at any time be removed from the Library, without the written consent of the Library Committee.

2. No manuscript in the Library, nor any paper read or address delivered before the Society, and deposited in the Library, shall be published, under the auspices of the Society, except by direction of the Board of Trustees.

3. The hours during which the Library shall be open shall be determined, from time to time, by the Library Committee.

4. During such hours, any Member of the Society may have free access to the Library, to consult any book or manuscript, except such as may be prohibited by the Board of Trustees, and to make excerpts from the same. Any person, not a Member, may obtain the like privilege from the Librarian, or upon the recommendation in writing of some Member. But no person, not a Member, shall be permitted to make excerpts from the manuscripts of the Society, excepting donors or depositors of the same, without the consent of the Librarian.

5. It shall be duty of the Librarian, or the assistant, to report to the Library Committee any injury done to any book or manuscript, by any person consulting the same; and for such injury, the person doing it shall make such compensation as the said Committee shall judge proper; and if he is not a Member, the said Committee shall have the power to prohibit him from further

access to the Library, and to prosecute him publicly if they deem it advisable.

6. The Librarian shall have charge of the Library and Cabinet of the Society, subject to the foregoing regulations, and subject also to the direction of the Library Committee. He shall keep a record of all donations and accessions to the Library and Cabinet, and report the same to the Society at each Annual Meeting.

XII. These By-Laws may be altered or amended by an affirmative vote of two-thirds of the Members present at any Meeting of the Society, provided such alterations or amendments shall have been proposed in writing to the Board of Trustees or to the Society at least two months previous to such Meeting; and such alteration or amendment shall not take effect, unless approved in writing by two-thirds of the Board of Trustees.

To facilitate the operation of the Revision of the Constitution and By-Laws of the New Jersey Historical Society, and to avoid possible complication over the question of the terms of office of the present Officers and Members of Committees—

Resolved, That the next Annual Meeting of the Society shall be held on Wednesday, October 27, 1897, at the Prudential Building, Newark, at eleven o'clock, A.M.

Resolved, That at said next Annual Meeting, the said Revised Constitution and By-Laws shall take effect at the call for Miscellaneous Business, and the election of Trustees shall then be held.

Resolved, That the time and place for the first Meeting of the Trustees elect, within thirty days after such Annual Meeting, shall be fixed by the President of the Society, and the notices thereof shall be mailed (one' week in advance of such first Meeting), to each of the Trustees elect, by the Corresponding Secretary.

Resolved, That upon the assembling of the Trustees elect for their first Meeting, all other existing offices and all Membership of Committees shall become and be vacant.

Resolved, That the Board of Trustees (when elected) may accept, from any person approved by them, a donation of a share of the capital stock of the Newark Library Association, in lieu of the payment of the sum of Fifty Dollars as a fee for Life Membership.

As a proper recognition of those whose patronage has been helpful to the Society—

Resolved, That the names of all persons, who heretofore at any one time have contributed One Thousand Dollars to the Society, shall be enrolled as Patrons.

The Committee recommend the printing, with the Revised Constitution and By Laws, the Act of 1846 incorporating the New Jersey Historical Society, the Act of 1856 increasing the limit of income, the Act of 1893 authorizing the extension of its Charter, and the Certificate filed for that purpose with the Secretary of State, also a list of the Society's Publications, copies of which are hereto attached.

>WILLIAM R. WEEKS, *Chairman*.
>JONATHAN W. ROBERTS,
>GEORGE S. MOTT,
>RICHARD F. STEVENS,
>JAMES E. HOWELL.

Dated May 20, 1897.

The foregoing Report was read at the Meeting of the Society, held at the Prudential Building, Newark, May 20, 1897, and the Constitution, By-Laws, Resolutions and Recommendations were adopted.

PUBLICATIONS

OF THE

New Jersey Historical Society.

Collections—Vols. I–VII, as follows:

Vol. I. East Jersey Under the Provincial Governments, by William A. Whitehead, 8 vo., pp. (V)+VI–VIII+(II)+341, with Maps and Plates, 1846.

Vol. I.—Second Edition, Revised and Enlarged, 8 vo., pp. (VII)+VI–VIII+(II)+486, with Maps and Plates, 1875.

Vol. II.—Life of William Alexander, Earl of Stirling, by his Grandson, William Alexander Duer, LL.D., 8 vo., pp. (IX)+XIV—XV+(II)+X—XII+272, with Portrait and Maps, 1847

Vol. III.—Provincial Courts of New Jersey, by Richard S. Field, 8 vo., pp. (VII)+VIII—XI+(I)+311+(I), 1849.

Vol. IV.—Papers of Lewis Morris, Governor of New Jersey from 1738 to 1746, 8 vo., pp. (V)+VI—VIII+(III)+XII—XXXII+336, with Portrait, 1852.

Vol. V.—Analytical Index to the Colonial Documents of New Jersey, in the State Paper Offices of England, compiled by Henry Stevens, edited by William A. Whitehead, 8 vo., pp. (V)+VI—XXIX+(III)+504, 1858.

Vol. VI.—Records of the Town of Newark, New Jersey, from its Settlement in 1666 to its incorporation as a City in 1836, 8 vo., pp. (V)+VI—X+294, with Map, 1864.

Vol VI.—Supplement—Proceedings Commemorative of the Settlement of Newark, New Jersey, on its Two Hundredth Anniversary, May 17, 1866; with Genealogical Notices of the First Settlers of Newark, by Samuel H. Congar; 8 vo., pp. (9)+10—182, 1866.

Vol. VII.—The Constitution and Government of the Province and State of New Jersey, with Biographical Sketches of the Governors, from 1776 to 1845, and Reminiscences of the Bench and Bar, by L. Q. C. Elmer, LL.D., 8 vo., pp. (V)+IV—V+(II)+VIII+(I)+2-6 +495, 1872.

New Jersey Archives, Vols. I–XVIII.
Index to Archives, (Vols. I–X.), in one volume.

The Proceedings of the Society comprise twenty-two octavo volumes, in paper covers, divided into two series, the first of ten volumes, the second of twelve volumes.

CPSIA information can be obtained
at www.ICGtesting.com
Printed in the USA
LVHW080808051218
599325LV00003B/255/P